To:
Enjoy

Flavors of Friendship

Celebrate your
Flavors of Friendship.
They May be
Life Savers!
Zonya Brewton
02-28-2009

Zonya Brewton

To:

_____

From:

_____

Thanks for being my friend.

© 2008 Zonya Brewton
All Rights Reserved.
Illustration of "Coffee Cups" courtesy of Corinthia B. King

No part of this publication may be reproduced, stored in a retrieval system, or transmitted, in any form or by any means, electronic, mechanical, photocopying, recording, or otherwise, without the written permission of the author.

First published by Dog Ear Publishing
4010 W. 86th Street, Ste H
Indianapolis, IN 46268
www.dogearpublishing.net

ISBN: 978-159858-810-1

This book is printed on acid-free paper.

Printed in the United States of America

Table of Contents

Preface i
Dedication vii
Introduction ix

1. Flavors of Friendship 1

2. My Friends 6

3. Eternal Friend 14

4. Full Circle Friend 20

5. Unexpected Friend 26

6. Yesterday Friend 30

7. Just as you are Friend 36

8. Different From Me Friend 42

9. Angel Friend 46

10. Glass Half Empty Friend 50

11. Seasonal Friend 54

12. Wind Beneath My Wings Friend 58

13. My Praying Friend 62

14. My Salon Friend 66

15. My Sister Friend 70

16. My Mother Friend 74

17. My Right Time Friend 78

18. My Opposite Gender Friend 82

Ideas for maintaining friendships 85

References 87

Preface

In today's society, many obligations keep me from staying connected with the people that life has drawn me away from. The lack of connection in no way represents a lack of desire on my part to communicate with my long-time friends. Many times an old friend will cross my mind, and just before I pick up the phone I'm distracted by another one of my "duty calls." Then a day turns into a month, and a month into a year and I have yet to make that phone call.

I often think about the different friends in my life that I've laughed with, cried with, and just plain enjoyed. Although it is hard to stay connected regularly to all of my friends, God has a way of making sure that I have the friend that I need at that time.

As I sit down to write this book I think about friends – past, present and future. I think about friendships that I will never have again. I think about two of my friends, Regina and Anita, who passed in May of 2006 with cancer, and I remember how much I valued our friendship.

I am fortunate enough to have a wide range of friends who, throughout the course of my life, are there at different times and for different reasons. I believe that in return I fill a particular friendship need for them as well.

As you read this book, I believe that you will be able to reflect on similar friendships and realize that our lives are enriched by each experience. This book is intended to encourage us to appreciate all of our friendships in their many flavors, and to realize that, at some point in time and in some situations, we are those friends.

The flavors of friendship are not unique but universal. I believe that we all can recognize someone in each of the chapters. We might even recognize ourselves, as I have. I have chuckled at some of the friendships and I have chuckled at myself.

How boring this world would be if we had only one flavor of friendship!

I hope that this book will encourage each of us to not only appreciate our friendships but to be the best friend that we can be.

Dedication

I dedicate this book to Regina, my eternal friend who departed this life in May of 2006, and to Anita, a colleague and friend who preceded her in February of the same year. Both were courageous souls and dedicated friends who battled cancer valiantly.

I also dedicate this book to all my friends who reflect many of the flavors in this book. I thank all my friends who support me daily through all of my trials and accomplishments. I thank you for tolerating me throughout our friendship and for accepting me for me. I thank you for forgiving me when I need forgiveness, for encouraging me when I need encouragement, and listening when I just need an ear.

Each of you in your own way supports me when I need support the most. You cause me to laugh when I am at the point of tears. You push me forward when I want to quit. When I think I am not enough, you remind that I am more than enough. In all of my imperfections, you accept me for who I am.

There are times when I feel defeated, but you remind me that "Greater is he that is in me, than he that is in theWorld." (KJV Bible, **1 John 4:4).** When I am too tired to pray, you pray for me.

Intro

I have no idea how I would have gotten through the last two years without my friends. I can truly say that I understand the phrase "it was the best of times, it was the worst of times." I am thankful that my friends were there for the challenges and the successes.

Over the years I have written many poems to celebrate a success or to encourage a friend in challenging times. As the words of encouragement poured from my heart to paper, in some way they returned as encouragement to me. I find it almost impossible to give without receiving.

Friendship is essential in the best and worst of times, whether realizing an achievement or struggling with a success. The absence of a friend is apparent when having no one to celebrate a birthday, a promotion or another major accomplishment with. Celebration usually implies more than one person. Friendship in the time of adversity is a blessing. The absence of friendship in adversity can feel like a curse.

Ecclesiastes 4:8-10   (New International Version)

8 There was a man all alone;
> he had neither son nor brother.
> There was no end to his toil,
> yet his eyes were not content with his wealth.
> "For whom am I toiling," he asked,
> "and why am I depriving myself of enjoyment?"
> This too is meaningless—
> a miserable business!

9 Two are better than one,
> because they have a good return for their work:

10 If one falls down,
> his friend can help him up.
> But pity the man who falls
> and has no one to help him up!

There are people who struggle with being a friend and as a direct result struggle with maintaining friendships.

"A man who has friends must show himself friendly"
Proverbs 18:24 King James Version

When people are not happy with themselves, their friendship can often prove to be the most challenging.

"Friendship with oneself is all-important because without it one cannot be friends with anyone else in the world."
- Eleanor Roosevelt

"If one is estranged from oneself, then one is estranged from others too. If one is out of touch with oneself, then one cannot touch others."
-Anne Morrow Lindbergh

I understand that every person that I come in contact with is not meant to be my friend, and that not every one of my friends have enough in common to be friends with each other. With the elimination of a mutual friend, many acquaintances would cease to exist.

Many a person has held close, throughout their entire lives, two friends that always remained strange to one another, because one of them attracted by virtue of similarity, the other by difference.
-Emil Ludwig

When I reflect on my different friendships, they are so diverse that it sometimes amazes me. I realize that each one of my friendships during different phases or events in my life fulfills a different role or need in my life. The best correlation I can think of for my different types of friendships is the different flavors of coffee. Therefore I refer to my friendships as the different flavors of friendship.

I laugh when I hear one friend say of another friend, "I can only take her in doses." I understand that comment. Just like coffee, sometimes you like a certain flavor but too much at one time might not be as enjoyable. Sometimes friendships are a lot like coffee, on a hot day you might prefer a refreshing cold coffee—on a cold day you might prefer a perky hot cup of coffee. There are days when I want/need a little extra flavoring in my coffee. Likewise there are some days when I prefer the company of a friend with a particular flavor. Enjoying a good friendship is like enjoying your favorite flavor of frappachino or latte.

At my regular coffee shop, as I approach, my order is recited before I speak. This is much like my closest of friendships. Most often I can predict how my closest friends will respond to a situation and consequently I understand how I need to manage my response to their situations. I could share the same situation with multiple friends and could predict the differences in their responses based on the different personalities.

I write this book to celebrate the different flavors of friendships in my life, for I truly gain something unique and useful from each and every one.

"Every person is a new door to a different world."
- from movie "Six Degrees of Separation".

Flavors of Friendship

CHAPTER 1

Flavors of Friendship

In order for friendships to develop, grow and be sustained there are some core characteristics that must be present. I'd like to reflect on some of the characteristics that I see and value most in my different Flavors of Friendships.

Characteristics of the Flavors of Friendship

Faithful to you
Longsuffering with you
Advocate for you
Values you
Objective when you need them to be
Respectful of you
Stands by you

Open-hearted with you
Forgiving of your mistakes

Fair to and with you
Regards your feelings
Impacts your life
Enjoys your company
Never wants to hurt you
Dedicated
Sensitive to your feelings
Hopeful for you
Impartial
Patient with you

<u>F</u>aithful
- *You do not see her on a regular basis, but she attends every celebratory event that you have.*

- *You can count on her when you are in a bind.*

<u>L</u>ongsuffering
- *She is patient and understanding when you are going through something and you seem to misplace your anger or grief.*

<u>A</u>dvocate
- *She will stand up and represent you when you are not there to represent or defend yourself.*

<u>V</u>alues
- *She values you and what you bring to her life.*

Objective
- *She is objective enough to share a different view with you.*

Respectful
- *She respects your views and opinions.*

Stands by You
- *She stands by you when no one else will.*

Openhearted
- *She shares honest expressions with you.*

Forgiving
- *She is willing to forgive your mistakes and understand that we all make them.*

Fair
- *She is fair in all her dealings with you.*

Regards your feelings
- *She will not tell you something that will hurt you unless she believes that the benefit of telling you will outweigh the pain.*

Impacts your Life

- *She is a positive influence in all areas of your life.*

Enjoys your Company
- *She will not dread spending a day with you, but will look forward to seeing you.*

Never wants to hurt you
- *She is considerate and will never hurt your feelings intentionally.*

Dedicated
- *She is dedicated to the friendship and will do everything she can to make it work.*

Sensitive to your feelings
- *She is sensitive when talking about topics that make you uncomfortable.*

Hopeful for you
- *She shares in your hopes and dreams.*

Impartial
- *She will talk to you honestly and give her unbiased view.*

Patient
- *She is patient with you, recognizing that God is not finished with you or her.*

My Friends

CHAPTER 2

My Friends

This chapter honors all my friends in various roles they have played in my life.

Although there are various characteristics of a friend, they will manifest themselves in different behaviors exhibited by those friends. We need to recognize when someone is being a friend and when they are not.

- *A true friend will tell you the things you do not want to hear but need to hear.*

"A friend can tell you things you don't want to tell yourself."
-Frances Ward Weller.

- *A true friend will understand when you just need an ear.*

"The most basic and powerful way to connect to another person is to listen. Just listen. Perhaps the most important thing we ever give each other is our attention.... A loving silence often has far more power to heal and to connect than the most well-intentioned words."
- Rachael Naomi Remen

- A true friend will be happy for your successes even if she has just had a failure.

"Anybody can sympathize with the sufferings of a friend, but it requires a very fine nature to sympathize with a friend's success."
- Oscar Wilde

- A true friend will not tell you hurtful things when she knows that you cannot use the information to improve a situation or protect yourself.

"Except in cases of necessity, which are rare, leave your friend to learn unpleasant things from his enemies; they are ready enough to tell them."
- Oliver Wendell Holmes

- A true friend hates to see you hurting, even if she warned you in advance.

"A friend is someone, who upon seeing another friend in immense pain, would rather be the one experiencing the pain than to have to watch their friend suffer."
- Amanda Grier

- *A true friend will accept you for who you are.*

"A friend is one who knows us, but loves us anyway."
-Jerome Cummings

- *A true friend will not just hang around for the good times, but will hold you up through the bad times.*

"Lots of people want to ride with you in the limo, but what you want is someone who will take the bus with you when the limo breaks down."
-Oprah Winfrey

Sometimes I have received messages from my friends that were hard to hear. Even when I have not agreed with the message, I have recognized that the message was simply what they believed was true and that the message was intended to help and not harm.

It is important as friends for us to recognize when to talk and when to listen. Every phone call of distress that I receive does not require action on my part. Sometimes it is important for me to listen and encourage the caller when appropriate. I have one good friend - bless her heart - that starts commenting before I can get the situation out of my mouth.

There might be friendships that dissolve for various reasons, but as time goes on you recognize that your friendship is stronger than whatever separated you and you come together again as friends. When you miss a friendship that seems to have dissolved, you need to reach out and reconnect, working out the differences that separated you.

I have been in situations where I had to decide whether or not to share information with a friend. As a child, it was very common to go back and forth telling what this one said about the other. At a very early age, my mother clarified for me that I should never share anything that someone said about another person unless not sharing that information would bring harm to the targeted person in some way. I have always tried to limit what I share based on this advice. I found myself in a situation where I realized a friend was being set up to appear to be something that she was not. I knew that sharing this information would hurt the friend, but not sharing it could ruin her reputation. I made the choice to share the information, because she would be spared a greater level of pain.

"Except in cases of necessity, which are rare, leave your friend to learn unpleasant things from his enemies; they are ready enough to tell them."
- Oliver Wendell Holmes

True friendships, especially among females, are extremely important. When women come together to share they will gain support and strength from other women who can empathize with their situation. I believe that friendships are crucial. I cannot imagine my life without my 'Girlfriends'.

Many times we isolate ourselves from friendships because of negative situations that have occurred with women we believed were friends but they intentionally hurt us. I have been burned by these types of relationships as well. Unfortunately, there are women who, for many reasons, are insecure and will not be happy for your success. We cannot let a bad friendship keep us from the friendship that God wants to bless us with.

I have had friends who were having a really rough time, but they stepped up and celebrated successes that I was having in spite of their trials. In the midst of their failures they were able to find joy in the success of a friend. When a true friend says, 'Well, I'm glad that at least one of us is having fun," she really means it.

Once in my life I was dealing with a court case, a situation at work, a fire in my kitchen, and the theft of my car. One event seemed to follow the other. When I spoke to my friends about my ordeals, I could hear the pain in their voices. If I did not know any better, I would have thought they were challenged by these situations, too. Friends share a love for you that at times will make your pain feel almost like their pain. When I talked to one friend about the theft of my car, she actually said, "Lord, we can't take anymore." She said that she felt as if this was her life.

I always want to be able to recognize and cherish the true friendships in my life.

HOW DO I RECOGNIZE YOU, MY FRIEND?

*How do I recognize
You, my friend?
You've been there through hard times,
Through thick and through thin.*

*You've celebrated my accomplishments,
With no envy in sight.
You've cheered me on,
With sheer delight.*

*You've stood in the shadows,
While I took the floor.
You've taken so little,
But given much more.*

*You've supported me
And encouraged my dreams.
You've lent me a shoulder,
On which to lean.*

*Even though you'd never
Experienced my pain,
You helped me weather the storm,
As though you felt the rain.*

*Your words were not always
What I wanted to hear,
But they were the words of my friend,
So true and so dear.*

*When my judgment was poor,
You helped me to see
A better way
To a better me.*

This poem is written
For each of you,
Who has been a friend,
So loyal and true.

For to be a friend,
Is a priceless treasure;
By giving of your heart,
You bring so much pleasure.

Let all of us,
As we kneel to pray,
Thank God for our friends,
Each and every day.

Eternal Friend

CHAPTER 3

Eternal Friend

"With every friend I love who has been taken into the brown bosom of the earth a part of me has been buried there; but their contribution to my being of happiness, strength and understanding remains to sustain me in an altered world."
- Helen Keller

As I approach the end of my 40s, I have become painfully aware that the friendships you take for granted can, in an instant, be gone forever with no possibility of return.

I met Regina in 1985 in the workplace; she was my trainer. When I first met her, I was turned off by her abruptness; but out of convenience, we became friends as we worked and lunched together. Initially I did what most people do: I judged "a book by its cover." Regina was very abrupt and direct. If she wanted to know something, she would ask you and if she wanted to tell you something she would. If she thought something you did was ridiculous she would tell you.

Regina left the company five years later in 1990. Since we no longer worked together, staying connected required a lot more effort. So we simply did not. I went to lunch with other friends, and life went on separately for Regina and me.

I spoke to Regina only occasionally over the next six years, but in 1996 motherhood brought us back together. She had a son in 1995 and I had a daughter in 1996. One thing that I am sure of is that a change in life will bring a change in friends. Once my daughter was born, spending time with my friends who had no children was a lot more difficult. I did not enjoy their company any less, but my focus was now different. Thus Regina and I joined together in our common bond of motherhood.

Even though I had known Regina for years before the birth of our children, I would have to say that our true connection came when we became parents. We now had a common goal and a common dream that would not change. We were focused on our children. Regina and I planned many activities together, including vacations, and I even joined a real estate business venture with her. We communicated several times a day, sometimes about our children, sometimes the business, and sometimes our common spiritual beliefs.

In 2004 Regina was diagnosed with breast cancer. She was healthy for a year but then developed what the doctors said was an unrelated brain tumor. We talked and prayed together constantly during her illness; however, I never expected her to die. Unfortunately Regina lost her battle to cancer in May of 2006.

Regina had some flaws (as we all do), but I discovered that once I looked past her sometimes abrupt exterior and saw her heart, I knew that she was a friend anyone would have been privileged to have. Regina did not call many people her friends, but if you were fortunate enough for her to consider you a friend, then you were truly blessed. Regina was a true and loyal friend who always looked for ways to help make life better for the ones she loved.

Regina's death reminded me of the importance of picking up the phone and calling your friends when they cross your mind, or sending a note at Christmas time to say hello.

We all have friendships on different levels, and staying in touch regularly with every friend who touches our lives is sometimes impossible. I realize though that because I have not spoken to a friend in three months does not make her any less of a friend than the one whom I speak to every day.

If you have never experienced the death of a dear friend, you should consider yourself fortunate. For those of you have experienced the loss of a friend, I empathize. For our friends who have departed they will forever be our eternal friends.

It is no doubt that with each friend that I have lost my world has been changed forever. I will forever be thankful for their contribution to my life that sustains me in this altered world.

My Eternal Friend

God gives us friendships
For so many reasons,
Some for a lifetime
And some for but a season.

Your time on this earth
Has come to an end,
But I'll never forget
My eternal friend.

We laughed and we cried,
We argued and agreed;
Sometimes you'd follow
And sometimes you'd lead.

I held your hand tight
Not wanting to let go,
But the time had come
And I knew it was so.

As I whispered in your ear,
Good bye my eternal friend,
I'll forever cherish our memories
Until we meet again.

Full Circle

CHAPTER 4

Full Circle

"Those truly linked don't need correspondence. When they meet again after many years apart, their friendship is as true as ever."
-*Deng Min-Dao.*

"The most beautiful discovery true friends make is that they can grow separately without growing apart."
-*Elizabeth Foley*

Sometimes our friendships undergo several transitions but in the end you realize that you have come full circle.

My best childhood friend and I traveled different paths. In adulthood our paths seemed to reconnect. I went off to college and my childhood friend went to college in our home town. During this time our lives took on very different meanings. She married while in college and started a family, while I remained single and started a career after college. I would visit her occasionally on my trips home. As her children got older, we began to talk more frequently; and now that her children are grown and moved away from home, we now speak several times a week.

This is an example of a relationship that changed as we both went through different phases in our lives, but the inconsistency of communication never changed the fact that we were friends. Friendships are not defined by how often you talk or the frequency of your visits but by what you feel in your hearts for each other.

There are very special childhood friends that I lost contact with but in times when they needed me I was there. It's not always convenient to be there when a friend needs you, but how much of an effort you put forth depends on the level of your friendship.

A very good friend's father passed away and the funeral was on my daughter's birthday. The celebration of my daughter's birthday was actually occurring the week after her birthday and so I made a one day roundtrip out of town to show my support for my friend during the time of her loss.

In another instance I was eight months pregnant with my daughter when my best college friend lost her mother. I really wanted to attend, but the funeral was a six hour drive away. I had been instructed by my doctor not to fly anymore at that point, and so considering the safety of my unborn child I decided not to attend the funeral. Instead I wrote a poem to be read at the funeral. My friend understood the situation and that I would have been there if the circumstances were different.

A very special friend was marrying for the first time at the age of fifty. Although we did not communicate regularly, I made a one day round trip to attend her wedding. Attending her wedding meant that I would be traveling for four consecutive weekends. I made the effort because I wanted to support this special occasion.

Although we may not see our childhood friends on a regular basis, I know that for special occasions or when they need us, that true friendship will make a true effort to be there.

My Full Circle Friend

We became friends as children
Oh so long ago,
Where the road would lead us
We truly did not know

We were the best of friends
There was never any doubt
If one of us was included
The other could not be left out

As our childhood ended
And we went our different paths
Was it just a childhood phase
Or would our friendship last

We'd reconnect on occasion
Being reminded of the past
We'd share some childhood stories
And certainly some laughs

As Adults we understand
That many things have changed
Though we reflect on our past
There we won't remain.

We started out as friends
Traveled different paths
Now we've come full circle
We're back again at last.

Unexpected Friend

CHAPTER 5

My Unexpected Friend

"Depth of friendship does not depend on length of acquaintance."
-Rabindranath Tagore

"Fear makes strangers of people who would be friends."
-Shirley MacLaine

Sometimes God places people in our lives for a specific reason and for a season. Sometimes friendships are created and sometimes they simply happen.

In order to have a friend it is important that we show ourselves friendly. Often we find ourselves in positions where we allow expectations to deprive us of a friendship that we could have had.

How many people have you heard say or maybe you have even said yourself, that, in a different time and place, they might have been able to be friends with a specific person?

I had an opportunity once to say, "in a different time and a different place we might have been friends." I was placed in a situation where I was able to meet someone who was very pleasant, kind, and considerate. The situation might have precluded us from being friends if I had closed my mind to the possibility.

A lady that my daughter was introduced to through her father would eventually become my friend. In this situation my daughter was crazy about her and I could see why. She was most humble and caring around me and to my daughter. Although I thought she was a wonderful person I did not anticipate the close friendship that we would eventually have.

As times passed, there were occasions when I needed to connect directly with this young lady who would be hosting my daughter at an event. Because we both had genuine respect and admiration for each other, the friendship developed. A few people commented, "Well, that is just strange that the two of you would be friends." I would always acknowledge that although it might appear odd to some people, I could see how it occurred.

I believe that God placed each of us in the other's path for a reason. We have supported each other in so many ways, both personal and business. Because we both showed ourselves friendly to each other we received true friendship. Our friendship was not created; it simply happened.

Through this experience I have learned a valuable lesson about friendship – Friendships will come from unexpected places if you keep an open mind.

My prayer is that as women we open up our minds and our hearts to potential friendships where we as women can support each other. Sometimes God places people in our lives for a specific reason and for a season. Sometimes friendship is created and sometimes friendship simply happens. Sometimes when you are not looking you might happen upon an unexpected friend.

My Unexpected Friend

Some people would say
We're the least likely friends;
They saw the beginning
But God knew the end.

Our first encounter
Was friendly and full of respect;
Neither of us was threatened
As some might expect.

You greeted me
With a heartfelt hug,
Not haughty or arrogant,
Not rude or smug.

The warmth from your spirit
It touched my heart;
I felt comfortable with you
Right from the start.

Some friendships happen
For a specific reason;
Some friendships are to last
But for a season.

We only know the beginning
But God knows the end;
Yet I know I'm thankful
For my Unexpected Friend.

Yesterday friend

CHAPTER 6

Yesterday

"True friendship is like sound health; the value of it is seldom known until it be lost."
- *Charles Caleb Colton*

"We call that person who has lost his father, an orphan; and a widower that man who has lost his wife. But that man who has known the immense unhappiness of losing a friend, by what name do we call him? Here every language is silent and holds its peace in impotence."
-*Joseph Roux*

"Too late we learn, a man must hold his friend
Unjudged, accepted, trusted to the end."
- *John Boyle O'Reilly*

Sometimes friendships end for reasons known and sometimes for reasons unknown. I have had friendships where things have happened and either one or both of us decided that it was something we could not get past. I understand that sometimes friendships are not always meant to be. Sometimes there is a common bond, but the differences cause the friendship to be too much effort.

It is possible to have a friendship that is so draining that it is best not kept. Severing the ties does not mean that you do not care for or love the person, but that a friendship that is detrimental to one or both parties is best left in the past.

I have heard several people say they have no idea what happened between them and a friend, that she just stopped returning their calls and after so many calls they stopped calling, too. It is unfortunate that sometimes friendships end and we never know why, but it is healthy to address the causes and move on.

I ended a friendship because I felt it could be detrimental to me and my daughter. After a party that I had given for my daughter, I received phone calls from various friends who shared comments that were out of line that one friend made to them about me, my daughter and her father. I approached this friend with the accusations, but she denied the comments. However, similar comments from other friends confirmed the statements and I decided that this friendship had to be left in the past.

I have experienced other situations in which someone would be friends with me this year and the next year they would not. Sometimes I suspected the reason and sometimes I had no clue. I know that sometimes people will have disagreements and not speak for a while; sometimes they get over it and sometimes they do not. Relationships that go back and forth become too high maintenance for me. Even when the person was a good friend, very supportive, and very uplifting, I just could not manage an on and off friendship. Sometimes you want to be friends with a person because you enjoy their company and value their ideas, but the friendship is so unpredictable that it is detrimental to your well-being. In these cases I try to see the good in the friendships and remember those times. Sometimes you just have to say I love you, I care about you but I have to deal with you on a different level, and sometimes not at all.

Friendships are usually forged out of common bonds, but sometimes we have to walk away, still loving our friends, but putting the friendship in the past.

My Yesterday Friend

*We made a decision
That we would be friends;
Irreconcilable differences
Brought it to an end.*

*I respected our friendship
As I'm sure you did too;
But it was too hard for me
And too hard for you.*

*So as we realize that our
Paths had to part.
It doesn't change how
We feel in our hearts.*

*I'll always respect you
As the friend that I knew;
I'll always give you
Credit that you are due.*

*As we move forward
Let's not look back with regret;
Let's remember the good times
And neither of us forget.*

*I'll always remember
My yesterday friend,
Even after our friendship
Has come to an end.*

Just as you are

CHAPTER 7

Just as You Are

"A friend is one who knows us, but loves us anyway."

- Fr. Jerome Cummings

"Your friend is the man who knows all about you, and still likes you."
- Elbert Hubbard

When a friend annoys me, I have to step back and remind myself that we all have our own personalities and differences. I have to realize that in the same way someone has annoyed me I have annoyed someone else as well. I have to remember that none of us are perfect and that we cannot expect perfection from our friendships.

I used to feel guilty when I had negative thoughts about a friend's personality. What I later realized was that it was natural to have these feelings, I could embrace them and determine how I could deal with that type of personality. There are many different personalities in friendships; if you have a broad enough range of friends, then you may encounter most of them.

The friend who is the "glass half empty friend" will always see the worst in any situation that you discuss with her. But you must be strong enough so that this doesn't impact you negatively. When a situation really has me down I do not discuss challenging situations with this type of friend.

The "glass half full" friend is open and receptive. She can always see the best in any situation. One caution to think about is that because she is so optimistic she may overlook some of the pitfalls that the "glass half empty friend" might see.

The fix it friend always want to direct you in what you should and should not do; rather than encourage or influence you she tries to direct your life. If you don't want direction then you might reconsider sharing with this friend. Or you have to be strong enough to accept the feedback but go forward doing what you know you need to do for yourself.

"When we honestly ask ourselves which person in our lives means the most to us, we often find that it is those who, instead of giving much advice, solutions, or cures, have chosen rather to share our pain and touch our wounds with a gentle and tender hand. The friend who can be silent with us in a moment of despair or confusion, who can stay with us in an hour of grief and bereavement, who can tolerate not knowing, not curing, not healing and face with us the reality of our powerlessness, that is a friend who cares."
-Henri Nouwen

Then there is the nurturer and encourager, who helps you be better than you are. She encourages you to reach for your dreams, try new things and step out on faith. She always has something positive going on in her life and so just being around her motivates you..

Just as You are

No person is perfect
So don't expect your friend to be.
I can't expect perfection from my friends
And they can't expect it from me.

Friendship is about accepting
Friendships for the good and the bad.
Sure you won't always agree with them
And sometimes they'll even make you mad.

Sometimes with your opinions
Your friends will not agree.
Allow them the opportunity
To think differently.

If you know the things about them
That make your blood boil.
Then stay away from those situations;
They are like water and oil.

There has got to be a reason
That you became friends.
Try to remember that reason;
Let it be what matters in the end.

No person is perfect
So don't expect your friend to be.
I can't expect perfection from my friends
And they can't expect it from me.

Different from Me

CHAPTER 8

Different from Me

"To cement a new friendship, especially between foreigners or persons of a different social world, a spark with which both were secretly charged must fly from person to person, and cut across the accidents of place and time."
-Cornelia Otis Skinner

Sometimes we limit our friendships when we are not comfortable or secure enough to cross different cultures, religions, races and genders, and yes opinions.

When I was younger, my friendships were formed with people of a similar culture and race as I am. As I got older, I began to realize that friendship is created in the heart and hearts are the same regardless of the culture, religion or race that you are.

Being employed by a global organization I have had the privilege of encountering people from all across the world, with various backgrounds. I have enjoyed learning of different cultures and have appreciated the uniqueness in all of them. Over the years I have forged friendships with people whom I have never met.

Flavors of Friendship

Of my ten closest friends, three of them are of a different race. Our friendship was not created because of our similarities or our differences, but they were created out of our respect and caring for each other. I am as close to these three friends as I am to the friends of my same race. There are for sure some things that we do not always understand about each other, but we share a mutual respect.

We also all have a core set of values. These values are the foundation that keeps us from hurting each other intentionally and that ensures our support and respect for each other. These values help us to recognize that, even if we do not always understand each other's world, we still appreciate each other's friendship.

Different from Me

I'm glad that we're different
Exposing each other to something new,
Through my experience you learn from me
Through your experience I learn from you.

True friendship isn't based
On the color of our skin-
True Friendship isn't even based
On what neighborhood we live in-

True friendship isn't based
Our what country you are from-
There are many things it's based on
But it is from the heart it comes.

True friendship isn't based on
How much exposure we have had-
Some people do believe that,
And that is truly sad.

True friendship isn't based on
Having a title behind one's name-
Because at the end of the day
Our basic needs are the same.

Friendship embraces the differences
And the similarities too.
It allows me to be me
And you to be you.

If we were just alike
How boring it would be!
I'm thankful for my different friend
That God has given to me.

Angel Friend

CHAPTER 9

Angel Friend

For he will command his angels concerning you to guard you in all your ways;
-Psalm 91:11

For it is written: He will command his angels concerning you to guard you carefully.
-Luke 4:10

Do not forget to entertain strangers, for by so doing some people have entertained angels without knowing it.
-Hebrews 12:2

Sometimes we are fortunate enough to encounter a friend who we are sure is one of God's angels.

I have one such friend whom I talk to occasionally. I have always told her that she must be one of God's angels. I first met her years ago at my place of employment.

At the time she was having a lot of female problems and it was unlikely that she would be able to have children of her own.

Yet, she was always the first to baby-sit for any of her friends; she also worked with children in foster homes, and even took in some foster children for a short time when they were required to leave the system because of their age and they had nowhere to go. She was always mentoring kids.

When she married, she ensured that her husband was significantly involved in the lives of his children from a previous marriage. When she realized that she and her husband could provide a healthier and safer environment for his children, she encouraged him to seek custody of them. She never felt insecure or threatened by their presence; but she helped to create a safe and loving environment for everyone, even her own adopted son.

I came to admire and respect her when I learned of her caring spirit, and through our love for children our friendship was born. I do not always talk to her, but it seems that every time I am going through some challenges in my life, I will get a phone call from her saying she was thinking of me. I eventually share with her what is going on with me, and she is, as always, positive and encouraging. I can truly say I have never heard her utter a discouraging word on any situation; she always focuses on the positive.

I often wonder how she knows just when to call and just what to say. The only explanation I have is that she is my Angel Friend.

My Angel Friend

You're one of God's Angels
I know that it's true;
You're always giving to others
It's just what you do.

Yes, God has Angels
In human form too;
You don't need to have wings
For him to use you.

God whispers in your ear
That someone needs you;
And then you his angel,
Are off to the rescue.

You follow your heart
And you always do what's right;
That's why God can use you
For others to see your light.

I'm thankful for my angel
That will suddenly appear;
But as quickly as she comes,
She will disappear.

I'm certain you're an angel-
It's the only explanation there can be;
I'm thankful that God assigned
This Angel to me.

Glass Half Empty Friend

CHAPTER 10

Glass Half Empty Friend

"Except in cases of necessity, which are rare, leave your friend to learn unpleasant things from his enemies; they are ready enough to tell them."
- Oliver Wendell Holmes

As I write this chapter about the glass half empty friend, I do not intend to portray any negativity. I write this with love. As you read this chapter you can probably think of a friend who will look at a glass and see it as half-empty rather than half-full. Positive thinking does not always come easy to everyone. Sometimes even I find myself thinking the worst and not the best of a situation.

I have a friend whom I love dearly and I believe she has my best interest at heart. However, if I share anything with her she will say at least one negative thing before she says something positive. For example if I say that I am going to drive across the country she would say, "I hope you don't run out of gas, and I hope this trip doesn't break you, because you know when you get back you might have lost your job." Her last comment will be, "Well, I know you are going make it because you usually succeed at whatever you try." At this point I am so bewildered by the first comments that I find it hard to appreciate the end compliment.

Sometimes I appreciate this friend, because she forces me to think about the pros and the cons of my escapades. Sometimes I have not played out the worst case scenario and I need to. Even in instances when I have already considered my options, I realize that she wants to ensure that I have covered all angles.

When communicating with this friend I decide when and what I will share with her. Sometimes I purposely call her because I want someone who is going to walk through the worst case scenarios. So I listen intently and let my faith be my guide.

My Glass Half Empty Friend

I'm thankful for
My Glass Half Empty friend.
You help me think it through
From beginning to end.

You don't allow me to ignore
A possible negative outcome,
If I only want to hear the good
Then you're not the one.

When sharing things with you
I should have thought it through,
Not only thinking of the positive
But of the negative, too.

Once you're sure I understand
All possible outcomes,
Then you'll align yourself
With where I'm coming from.

There is much that I've gained
Having you as my friend.
With a word of caution you will start
But with encouragement you will end.

Seasonal Friend

CHAPTER 11

My Friend for a Season

"Some people come into our lives and quickly go. Some stay for awhile and leave footprints on our hearts. And we are never, ever the same."
- Anonymous

I understand that every person that comes into my life is not meant to be my best friend, and every friend that comes into my life is not meant to stay. I believe that there are people who come into our lives for a season; they may come for a season, leave for a season, and return for a season. They might come for a season leave and never return.
- *(KJ, Isaiah 46:10 Jeremiah 8:7)*

What is important to realize is that friendships sometimes end, not due to any fault of either friend, but due to circumstances - it is just time to move on.

I have had friends who were going through or had gone through similar things that I was experiencing to come into my life. We were there to encourage each other. I think back on some of those friendships and will always remember that God brought them into my life at a time when I needed them most, and when that season ended, He sent us both to another place where we were needed.

Have you ever noticed that although you have some friends forever you constantly have some friends who rotate in and out of your life, as the seasons change?

"If a man does not make new acquaintance as he advances through life, he will soon find himself left alone. A man, Sir, should keep his friendship in constant repair."
- Samuel Johnson (1709 - 1784) British lexiographer.

I am just as thankful for my seasonal friends as I am for my friends who seem to have been with me for a lifetime.

My Friend for a Season

I'm thankful for your friendship
If only for a season;
We thought it was by chance
But God knew the reason.

We only knew the beginning
But God also knows the end.
He knew that we would need
Each other for a friend.

There is a time for the seasons
And sometimes for our friends;
It doesn't mean we'll never share
Those friendships again.

Even the stork in the sky;
Knows her appointed season.
The rain falls from the sky-
Even it has a reason.

So I'm thankful for my friendship
For this appointed season;
We thought it was by chance
But God knew the reason.

Reference:
Isaiah 46:10

Jeremiah 8:7

Wind Beneath my Wings

CHAPTER 12

Wind Beneath my Wings Friend

"Two are better than one; because they have a good reward for their labour. For if they fall, the one will lift up his fellow: but woe to him that is alone when he falleth; for he hath not another to help him up."
-Bible: Ecclesiastes

"Treat people as if they were what they ought to be and you help them become what they are capable of being."
-Goethe

"In everyone's life, at some time, our inner fire goes out. It is then burst into flame by an encounter with another human being. We should all be thankful for those people who rekindle the inner spirit. "
-Albert Schweitzer

Flavors of Friendship

I thank God for the wind-beneath-my-wing friends. Although I considered myself a person who soars, I know I need some wind beneath my wings. Sometimes it is easy to soar when there is little or no risk. But I have encountered a friend in my life who challenged me to be more than I ever thought I could be. She even challenged me to step outside of my comfort zone and to take a calculated risk. She assured me that she would support me in every way.

I will never forget a business deal that a friend brought to me. In order to be a part of this business deal, I had to take a significant amount of equity out of my house. She sat down with me, showed me the numbers, and helped me think through the best and worst case scenarios: I would make at least fifty percent profit on the money that I used or I would not make any money at all. I consider this venture a calculated risk and a little scary because I am usually a low-risk taker. When I saw the numbers and felt that the chances of succeeding were pretty high, I took this risk and the best case scenario came to pass. Because of the encouragement of my friend, I was able not only to make some significant improvements in my lifestyle but also to be a blessing to others.

The wind-beneath-your-wings friends always push you to do more than what you ever thought you could do and to be better than what you ever thought you could be. Friends like these are critical because they see your potential when you cannot and they believe in you, even when you do not believe in yourself.

My wind-beneath-my-wings friend left my side in May of 2006, but God already had other people in place to fill that role. In remembrance of my friend, I always try to be that supporting and encouraging person she was. I believe that when you help others reach their dreams, you will reach your dreams faster.

The Wind Beneath My Wings friend

When I thought I could go no higher
You were underneath my wings;
You knew that there was more,
I could accomplish greater things.

When the pressures that I felt
Started causing me to fall,
You were right there beside me,
Encouraging me to stand tall.

When I had a dream
I was frightened to pursue,
You wouldn't let me give up,
And I am thankful to you.

Things might have been different
If it had not been for you;
I wanted to stand outside the door,
But you pushed me through.

I'm thankful for you-
My wind beneath my wings;
I wanted you to know,
I'm now doing greater things.

My Praying Friend

CHAPTER 13

My Praying Friend

"For the eyes of the Lord are on the righteous And his ears are attentive to their prayer"
-Bible:1 Peter 3:12

I have a very good friend with whom I don't always see eye to eye, but one thing that I am sure of is that she prays for me always.

We have all been protected and brought through situations not only because of the petitions of a praying friend. A praying friend knows when you are at a point where you cannot even pray for yourself and so she will pray harder for you.

The bible requires us to pray for our enemies. Matthew 5:55 says, "But I tell you: Love your enemies and pray for those who persecute you." I know that I am not alone when I say praying for an unpleasant person is sometimes very difficult to do. In many instances as I prayed for my enemy, the persecution became so great that I found it challenging to continue this prayer. During this time my praying friend sensed the difficulty I was having and started praying for me to be able to pray again for my enemy. Because of my praying friend and her specific prayer, God did change my heart, and I began once again to pray for my enemy as God commands me to, and I saw things change for the positive.

You can be put on a prayer list for a specific prayer, but when you have a praying friend, she is going to pray beyond what even you know that you need. There were times when I was not able to pray effectively for myself, but things changed for me, not because of my prayers, but because of the prayers of my praying friend. (KJ, 1 Peter 3:12)

My Praying Friend

1 Peter 3:12

For the eyes of the Lord are on the righteous
And his ears are attentive to their prayer,
How wonderful it is to have a
Righteous praying friend who cares.

When I was in the valley
You saw me from the hill;
You didn't turn and walk away,
You prayed that "Peace Be Still."

You are my praying friend,
I know I'm always in your prayers
Because when I cannot pray,
God has put you there.

You intercede for me
Just when I need you to;
It's through the prayers of friends
that help me to go through.

You always pray for others
As God requires you to;
It's when you pray for others
That you receive your breakthrough.

When I was in the valley
You saw me from the hill;
I'm glad you didn't walk away
But prayed that "Peace Be Still."

My Salon Friend

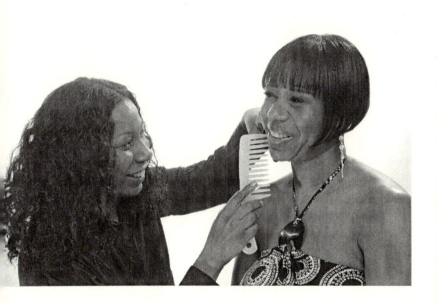

CHAPTER 14

My Salon Friend

"This communicating of a man's self to his friend works two contrary effects; for it redoubleth joy, and cutteth griefs in half."
- Francis Bacon

I know that most women feel good when they leave the hair salon. No matter the setting or the atmosphere, this is a place where you go and expect to leave looking and feeling better than when you went.

I know that there is a stereotype out there about hair salons being a place where ladies go to gossip. At least that is what you see on many movies with a beauty is some type of bond between the client and the hair stylist. .

I have two hair stylists and I can say that my experiences at their salons are truly uplifting and positive. When I go to either stylist, I leave feeling better not only on the outside but on the inside as well. We share our dreams and encourage each other to go for them.

My long-time hair stylist and friend is a Christian as well. Whenever we talk she encourages me spiritually. I wrote a poem for her stepmother, based on the feelings she shared about her. After I wrote the poem, my stylist continued to encourage me to write and publish my writing. She always sees the positive in every situation. So regardless of how I feel when I walk into the salon, I never leave feeling down.

My Salon Friend

*Once or twice a month
I come in to your shop
For a fresh hair do,
But that's not where it stops.*

*You beautify my hair
And you stimulate my mind.
It's the person that you are
So wonderful and kind.*

*From the time that I arrive
To the time that I leave,
We share words of encouragement
That we're both happy to receive.*

*We don't waste our time
With unfruitful conversation;
There is no idle talk
That goes on at your station.*

*When I'm feeling down
And I come into your shop,
I know you'll beautify my hair
But that is not where it will stop.*

*I'll leave feeling encouraged
And ready to take on the world;
That is why I love you,
My Salon Girl!*

My Sister – My Friend

CHAPTER 15

My Sister—My Friend

"Fate chooses your relations, you choose your friends."
- Jacques Delille (1738 - 1813) French poet.

I grew up in a family with five sisters. Of course my closest connections during these adolescent and teen years were with my sisters immediately below and above me in age. Our relationships were no different from what I have observed in other families then and now that I am older. I have often heard my mom and other parents comment that it appears their children do not even like each other. Because of some of our "uprisings," my mom thought many times that my younger sister and I were not related at all.

It is interesting to see siblings argue with each other and talk about each other but will not allow an outside person to do the same. Regardless of how siblings argue and fuss there is still a bond that they may be too young to recognize, but makes them stand up for each other.

The bond that you had in childhood often strengthens as you get older and become more mature and stop competing and arguing over things that become insignificant. It is at this time that you can walk across the bridge that is now developing between sisterhood and friendship. You realize how blessed you are to have a sister with whom you can actually bond as a friend.

My daughter, an only child, witnesses the bond between me and my sisters and comments that she is sad that she will never have a sister and will never be an aunt. I explained to her that she could acquire a sister and become an aunt through marriage. Sisters are not limited to blood.

This chapter is dedicated to all the sisters who argued as children and have bridged the gap between sisterhood and friendship.

My Sister - My Friend

I'm thankful you're my sister
But just as thankful you're my friend.
I can't really remember when the bridge
Between sisterhood and friendship began.

I think back on our childhood
How we were at each other's throat,
Sometimes over things as little
As who should have the remote.

We laughed and we played,
We argued and we fought,
Neither of us behaving
As we knew we had been taught.

We could argue with each other
A privilege between us two,
But no one else was allowed
To bother me or you.

Now we're all grown up
And the arguing has ceased,
In our older age
Our relationship is filled with peace.

I'm still thankful you're my sister
But just as thankful you're my friend,
I'm thankful we've grown up
And You're now my Sister-Friend.

My Mother – My Friend

CHAPTER 16

My Mother – My Friend

"What is a friend? A single soul in two bodies."
- Aristotle

There are various opinions on whether or not a mother can be friends with her child. I tell my daughter all the time that she is one of my best friends, but she knows that I am her mother first. When I tell my daughter that she is one of my best friends, she understands that the relationship is in a different context from that of my adult friends. A Mother and a daughter can have that special bond as if a single soul in two bodies and that is the relationship that allows friendship when the daughter becomes an adult.

There were discussions that I thought I would never have with my mother. My mother is a very strong Christian woman, lives by the words in the Bible. She believes that you should pray for those who despitefully use you. I remember calling her once to share a story about an acquaintance mistreating me. I expected her as my mother to be angry with the person, but as Christian she could not be. As a mother she felt my pain and hurt for me, but she spoke to me and counseled me, not as a mother, but as a friend.

After listening to my story, my mother told me that I had made my bed hard and I was going to have to lie in it. I am sure we have all heard this saying at some time. What she was telling me was that I was an adult and I made adult decisions, and as much as she hated what I was going through, I was going to have to live with the consequences of my choices. I believe that this was very hard as a mother to tell her daughter, but as a friend she had to tell me..

I shared this situation with my mother, but now I am sure that I shared it with a friend as well.

My Mother-My Friend

Whoever said you can't be
Both my Mother and my Friend,
Well maybe not when I was younger
But this is now and that was then.

You nurtured and you disciplined
Not trying to be my friend,
You were who you needed to be
So that in life I could win.

When I needed to talk you listened
With a Mother's ear,
Knowing that what I really needed
Was to have my Mother near.

Now I'm all grown up-
And you did your job well-
That you were an outstanding Mother
Is not hard to tell!

Your role of Mother
Will never ever end,
but as two adults
we can now be friends.

I'm thankful for my Mother,
I'm thankful for my Friend,
For one role to start
The other doesn't have to end.

Who ever said you can't be
Both my Mother and my Friend,
Well maybe not when I was younger.
But this is now and that was then.

Right Friend – Right Time

CHAPTER 17

Right Friend- Right Time

"Many a person has held close, throughout their entire lives, two friends that always remained strange to one another, because one of them attracted by virtue of similarity, the other by difference."
-Emil Ludwig

"Without wearing any mask we are conscious of, we have a special face for each friend."
-Oliver Wendell Holmes

"If a man does not make new acquaintance as he advances through life, he will soon find himself left alone. A man, Sir, should keep his friendship in constant repair."
- Samuel Johnson (1709 - 1784) British lexiographer.

I have a multitude of friends, of different levels of friendship and of different walks of life. I have some friends who regardless of how much they would like to, they cannot understand or relate to every situation that I am going through.

Flavors of Friendship

Thankfully, every friend and every friendship is not the same. It is because of the differences in our friends and our friendships that we have multiple friends that we can depend on and that can depend on us. I have experienced friends who had very limited friendships, and expected every need to be met by the one friend. I have found these friendships very challenging at times because it is very difficult to be what everyone needs when they need it.

Having multiple and diverse friendships is key in maintaining balance in your life. I have some friends who because of physical location I only converse with via phone and others that I can physically connect with if I need to talk or just get away. However, distance has never limited the ability of me and my long distance friends to support and be there for each other. We all know that we are each only a phone call away.

Because I have a multitude of friends from different walks of life, personalities, and levels of friendships, I know where to go when I want compassion, encouragement, or a swift kick in the behind. For each of these needs I would have to go to different places.

There is the friend that is challenged with showing compassion and there is the friend that is always compassionate. There is the friend that is talented at encouraging and the friend who is talented at challenging you when you need to be challenged. There is the friend that doesn't have the heart to tell you to stop complaining and get off of your behind and do something about it, and there is the friend that will tell you just that.

I am thankful to say that I have all these types of friends and I'm thankful that when I need them, I know just which one to call.

Right Friend - Right Time

I have a multitude of friends
I'm thankful for them all
When I'm at my lowest point
I know just who to call

I have a multitude of friends
Some live so far away
But if I need my distant friend
I can call her night or day

I understand the love
That my friend has for me
Regardless of the compassion
I think I fail to see

I understand my friend
Who wants me to consider all
She points out the downside
To help save me from a fall

I have a multitude of friends
Some are different as can be
I enjoy the differences
Between my friends and me

I have a multitude of friends
And I'm glad that they are mine
I'm glad I have the right friends
Just at the right time.

My Opposite Gender Friend

CHAPTER 18

My Opposite Gender Friend

"Friends are generally of the same sex, for when men and women agree, it is only in the conclusion their reasons are always different.
-George Santayana

Although this is mainly a book about my relationship with my girlfriends, this book would not be complete if I were not to mention my guy-friends. I am most thankful for my girl-friends, but I am equally thankful for my guy-friends. Some of my male friends have supported me for years and years through my triumphs and my trials. They have offered me a male perspective when I needed one.

I still have guy-friends today that allowed me to cry on their shoulders through failed relationship and jokingly volunteered to take care of the situation for me. These friends and their platonic relationships are priceless. People often tell me that guys cannot be platonic friends with females, but I believe that to be untrue. I believe that male friendships do exist and are essential to the balance that we all need in friendships.

A male friend whom I've known since high school only connects with me every few years; but each time that we connect, he and I are both excited to catch up on what has been going on in the other's life. When I walk away I know that it might be another year or two before we talk again, but I know that, at any time during that period apart, my friend is only a phone call away if I need him. When a male college friend heard about my first book, he reached out to me just to say hello. I had almost forgotten about our friendship, not having seen him since college some twenty five-years ago. That one conversation reminded me of why we had been friends in college and how much I missed our friendship.

All along my journey I have made male friends, some of whom I may not ever see again, and others with whom I may cross paths only occasionally. Then there are those friends with whom I will communicate just because of common situations or locations.

I am thankful for each one of my male friends because without their balance, my circle of friendships would not be complete.

My Opposite Gender Friend

I treasure our friendship
and your different point of view
You've been there for me
And I've been there for you

You have a different perspective
That I don't always understand
I have the view of woman
And you the view of a man

We have different discussions
Than that I have with my girls
Together we share a perspective
From a different view of the world

You've been there for so long
Through my triumphs and my trials
If you thought that I needed you
You would travel endless miles

I'm thankful for you my guy-friend
And your perspective that I need
Without your friendship
My circle would not be complete

Ideas for maintaining friendships

For various reasons, staying in touch with some friends might become challenging. Maybe they have small children, or live too far away. I am listing some ideas that have worked for me.

- Write down a list of friends that you would like to make contact with and how often you would like to make contact with them. Remember, if you do not make the effort then you will probably not stay in contact.
- I have friends that I try to get together with on a quarterly basis. In this instance, I take a couple of hours off from work at least once a quarter and we meet at Starbucks immediately after our children's carpool.
- There is another group of friends that I try to see on an annual basis. We usually attempt to have a gathering around Christmas time. If you tie it to a specific season then it can become a tradition and it will help people with planning.
- You can also start some type of interest group around a common topic so that you can visit with your friends and you can also share valuable information. Some friends and I are considering starting a real estate investing group, where we can come together on a common interest.

- Sending cards is a great idea when it seems that getting together is impossible. I have several friends that I keep in touch with through annual Christmas cards or some other special occasion. Some of these friends I have not physically seen for years.
- Picking up the phone and just calling a friend to say hello also works when you can't really find the time to get together. I have a friend that I rarely see but we speak on the phone on a regular basis.
- I know that we all need to exercise, and this is a great opportunity to spend time with a friend. I have often connected with friends just to go walking. I have most recently joined a morning boot camp that allows for me and a few of my friends to get together in the wee hours of the morning working toward a common goal.
- In an age of computers sending an electronic e-card is easy. There are so many sites that allow you to send electronic e-cards.
- I am not the best at keeping up with birthdays but I have friends who have used a new tool to remind them of birthdays so that they can make a phone call to say happy birthday or to send an electronic e-card.
- Create a book club with a few of your friends, allowing each one to invite one of their friends to join. This encourages new friendships. I'm not currently a part of a book club, but I'm told that twelve is a good number to limit your book club to.

References

I used many resources for my quotes. I would like to share some of the electronic resources that were used.

http://www.friendship.com.au/quotes/quofri.html

http://www.friendship.com.au/quotes

http://www.wisdomquotes.com/cat_friendship.html

http://www.quotedb.com/quotes/2920

http://www.indianchild.com/friendship_quotations.htm

http://www.best-quotes-poems.com/Friendship-Quotes.html

http://www.heartquotes.net/Friendship.html